WEALTHIER VERSION OF YOU

With simple mind shift

A Dedication . . . to My Father

My inspiration for writing this book was to make my parents feel proud and happy about me. Being a mother, I realize the hard work, dedication, commitment, and self-sacrifices they made for my sisters and me. My father passed away unexpectedly due to Corona in April 2021. He was a mentor, an idol, an inspiration, and much more to me. I remember how he made me feel special on my birthdays. I remember how he taught me English and introduced me to driving a scooter, a car, and many other things. Because of him, I had almost traveled all over the places in India with my family before marriage. He always used to help people. Hence, he was well-loved everywhere, and even after one year of his death, we are getting calls asking for "Tulsankar Saheb." I remember my parents' efforts to bring up the whole family. By God's grace me and my sisters are enjoying our mothers company n blessings, and she continues to support, and encourage us in every possible way. Although my father is no longer physically present in my life, I still feel his impact every day. I am dedicating this book to my father, Shri. Balkrishna Tulsankar to pay a small tribute to him.

Writing a book is harder than I thought and more rewarding than ever imagined. None of this would have been possible without the help of my sisters, the BTF team, and my colleague. I'm forever thankful for your insights and ongoing support in bringing my book live.

Preface

It's been a pleasure to share my life journey and experiences with all the readers through this great platform on our struggle towards financial freedom and achievement. But even after being successful, the economic freedom journey is like an ongoing process with lots of challenges, and I miss my father and his guidance a lot more than words. So here I am with my life journey after marriage because before marriage, life was easy, no liabilities and responsibilities, no struggles, with my parents' blessings. So this book is all about sharing personal experiences faced during the financial battle and the methodologies used to successfully conquer the financial freedom fight, which I expect all to follow in your life and taste the success of financial independence.

Soon after graduating in 2001, I worked for two private and three govt. Organizations. In 2005, while working as an assistant in an organization, I entered married life. To establish lifestyle stability, I decided to purchase a house to avoid regular shifting of place and being a tenant, with my husband's support. To support our dream, we needed a secondary income for which we planned to purchase a car and lent it to adjust the loan installments.

Consequently, we had taken housing loan & car loan simultaneously at the initial stage of our marriage. However, paying installments of both the loans from our income had become a nightmare. Although we had rented our car to a company, we had to bear fuel expenses, maintenance, and driver payment in advance, and in the subsequent month, the bill for car rent be disbursed. Managing our finances had become a horrible job. At times we were running with nil, and eventually, it turned out to non fulfillment of our basic needs.

Nevertheless, with the change in job and salary hike, we got some relief; however, we decided to streamline the finances by keeping the overall expenses at minimal and max balances for loan installments. We managed our finances meticulously to cover all the available loans at the earliest. We were keeping aside regular savings, bonus pay-outs, and yearly increments to repay the loan amount and release the burden of the loan at the earliest. With saving habits, we could scrape out a car loan in four years and a housing loan in six years. We both had made loads of efforts to improve our lifestyle and standard of living with many sacrifices, and as a result, we were able to pull out ourselves from draining in the swamp. However, many people can't and end up living a stressful life. Setting a financial goal, making consistent efforts, and sacrificing the comfort zone to achieve success; were the lessons we learned through the financial trouble.

I have seen many people, including my friends, colleagues, relatives, neighbours, or the people around, struggling to live a stress-free life. However, they cannot cope with challenges and finally live a regular stressful life leaving it to their destiny. They become fearful of the challenges they come across and do not take a little extra effort to transcend their lives, owing to fear of failure. They get stuck in a rat race and cannot come out of it. Many people walk on the same path throughout their lives without knowing where it's leading and ignore the rest possible pathways which may lead their lives to success.

Only a few people choose to walk on a different path without getting fearful of hurdles since they believe in creating their destiny and are super crazy about achieving their goals.

There are only 5% of people in the world who possess 95% of the total wealth, and the rest 95% of people in the world hold only 5% of the total wealth.

For that reason, my friends, to be on the list of those 5% people who possess 95% of the total wealth in the world, we need to think differently and act differently to get extraordinary results. But, by doing the same things repeatedly, we will be heading towards the same results we are getting today.

> *Money will come when you are doing the right thing. – Mike Phillips*

With this book, I want to make people unleash their inner power and explore various ways of making money; to bring out a successful and wealthier version of them. This book will take you through the journey of finding multiple ways to get rid of money challenges and become a wealthier version of yourself. The transformation in your lives will happen with simple mind shifts and invariable efforts. Stepping towards the goal with consistency in efforts is the only key to success.

So let's begin the journey with a commitment to transformation in your life with consistent efforts towards achieving the desired goals.

TABLE OF CONTENTS

Preface

Chapter 1. Does working hard at a job would make me rich?

Chapter 2. Why am I not able to manage my finances?

Chapter 3. How can I earn or grow money with my possessions?

Chapter 4. What are the passive income options?

Chapter 5. What is the secret behind the success of progressive people?

Chapter 6. Money Mind Block?

Chapter 7. The Success Mantra

Chapter 1. Does working hard at a job would make me rich?

Here is the story of two close friends working in a private organization, namely Seeta & Geeta. They both had completed graduation and joined as an assistant in an office together for ten years. As the years passed, Geeta improved her knowledge and skills as per the job requirements. She started working on her personality, joined various classes for personality development, and started reading relevant books to improve her knowledge. As a result, within ten years, Geeta got promotions in her company and currently working as a manager in the same company.

On the other hand, Seeta remained in the same post as she didn't get any promotion in 10 years of her career. She lives in a 1 BHK house that she bought three years ago, and both her husband and she were managing the home loan and other expenses somehow. However, due to Covid 19 crisis, her husband lost his job and started facing a lot of trouble with her finances; as a result, she could not pay her dues in time. Having scarce resources and money to run the house, her life has become miserable.

Once Seeta & Geeta were in a discussion:

Geeta: What happened, Seeta? You look worried.

Seeta: I am so worried, Geeta; I don't know how I can manage the expenses.

On the one hand, the day-to-day expenses have increased due to inflation, whereas our earnings are not growing in that proportion. On the other hand, I took a home loan three years ago, and about 80% of my earnings are being spent on the home loan installments, and only 20% of my income remains for daily needs for the month. Therefore, I have more liabilities as compared to my income. Whatever I earn disappears within 15 days, and in the next 15 days, I am left with hardly little money for my day-to-day expenses. I don't know what to do; I cannot manage my finances. I am tired of working it and not able to come out of this trap. I am very frustrated and want to cope with my financial issues as early as possible. Due to the scarcity of money me & my husband end up in arguments to find a reliable solution to get more money to meet our daily needs. As a result, our relationship is getting bitter. We are unable to fulfill our kid's wishes, and now fulfilling our wishes have become a dream.

Geeta, I find it very hard to make money. Money doesn't come to me quickly. However, I am amazed by your success. You have changed your life tremendously, whereas I am still struggling to achieve success in wealth and my position in this job. So please acquaint me with your secret to improving your life and finances so that I can also bring in changes in my life to become successful.

Geeta: Certainly, Seeta, I will tell you everything I know, and I follow but promise me one thing, that you will completely engross yourself in the process in such a way that there would be no alternative to the success.

Seeta: Unquestionably, please explain to me the process.

> *"Financial freedom is available to those who learn about it and work for it."* - Robert Kiyosaki, Rich Dad Poor Dad.

Geeta: When we joined together, we were just graduates. As I continued to do various jobs in this organization, I realized that I had to work on my knowledge and skills to achieve higher positions. I observed my senior officials and their working style and always tried to imbibe their qualities to bring improvement in me. So I started working on my skills and knowledge and developed a habit of allocating 10% of my income for self-improvement and investments.

Seeta: Self-improvement? How will that help one in improving their financial status?

Geeta: Self-improvement has changed my life significantly. As you know, I belong to a small village, and I have done my graduation in the local language, which is why I was hesitant to speak English due to my limited vocabulary and lack of fluency. My job required letter drafting and connecting with clients on various issues. Lacking English fluency made my job a very tough task for me. I started feeling inferior and realized that I would live the same mediocre life without self-improvement. Nevertheless, I decided to change the situation. I started reading various books on self-improvement, and in the meanwhile, I also started searching for English-speaking classes.

In a few days, I finalized a class close to my house with the intention that I could adequately handle my household chores after office and simultaneously managed to attend the English-speaking course. After office hours, I used to go to the classes directly and then home. Initially, it was a bit difficult for me to manage the time for study and classes, but I started working on it well over a while. I used to study whenever I was getting time. After doing that course, I started utilizing the knowledge gained at my job, and now I can speak English fluently and write English aptly. I have not only learned English speaking but also practiced with my family members, friends, and colleagues; as a result, my work turned out to be more effective. My senior officials started noticing it, which led me to get promotions in my job. Therefore, first of all, we need to start investing in ourselves to improve our knowledge and skills, which will lead us to success.

> "Formal education will make you a living; self-education will make you a fortune." - Jim Rohn, 7 Strategies for Wealth & Happiness.

Putting aside 10% of income for self-improvement may be difficult in the current situation; however it is necessary to level up ourselves to get better opportunities/promotions. One can decide how much to set aside from total income for self-improvement and investment. Additionally, we need to develop the inborn talents/skills, or we can create one, to get better opportunities in that area.

> "Pursuing your passion is fulfilling and leads to financial freedom." - Robert G. Allen, Creating wealth.

Chapter 2. Why am I not able to manage my finances?

Seeta continued: Geeta, you have explained to me on to improve my knowledge and skills, but how I would be able to handle my finances? A maximum part of my salary ends within 15 days on loan installments and the remaining on fundamental essentials; it's been tough for me to manage the finances? Even after working hard, I cannot raise more money to manage our expenses and liabilities. So making more money has become a challenging task for me to carry through.

Geeta: Dear, not all of us are fortunate enough to be born rich. However, we don't have to be lucky celebrities to get rich. Viewpoint varies when it comes down to what it means to be considered rich. Ultimately, the thing to remember is that being rich isn't just about the only money you accumulate but also matters about your net worth.

Net worth is calculated based on your assets and the liabilities you owe and is the balance aggregate from the expenditure. The next step could be planned out once we figure out the present net worth. The value of current net worth never matters; you may start from scratch to reach the destination, which means being wealthy with a few simple, achievable steps. Let's get into them!

1. Analyze your monthly expenses:

Write down your monthly expenses to identify the significant area of expenditure and categorize the expenses as per priority, such as daily needs, utility bills, health care, occasional shopping, travel, educational expenses, entertainment, etc. Once you figure out your expenses, cut down the expenses to a manageable proportion explicitly on nonessential or avoidable expenses to save on money. For example, cutting expenses on entertainment, eating out, expensive coffee, designer clothing, impulsive buying, etc., can support your savings. Living below your means should be a financial lifestyle one needs to apply to build and attain wealth.

2. Preparing a Budget with an Income & Expenses Statement:

Writing down your monthly expenses and liabilities plays a crucial role in budgeting. It holds you accountable for the money you spend. The budget is prepared to plan, organize, track and improve your financial situation. Getting on a budget is very essential when it comes to getting rich. It keeps you focused on your long-term financial goals by consistently controlling your spending and improving the saving and investing segment. You have to choose the best suitable budgeting plan that works for you and adhere to it. For preparing a budget, you have to prepare an income and expenses statement. Then, closely analyze the monthly outgoings, determine the fixed and variable expenses, and adjust the spending to save more for investments.

3. Minimize the expenses on unnecessary things – spend wisely:

You can minimize expenses by cutting down the outlay on unnecessary things. Consider a real-life example where a person has a mobile with sufficient output. He came across a newly launched mobile in the market with advanced features and considered buying it. However, before buying, he should ask himself, "Do I need a new phone just for advancement in features? Is my old phone not sufficient enough for fulfilling my requirements?". By doing this activity, he would realize whether he needs an advanced mobile phone or it is just an impulsive purchase. He must go for a new phone only when he considers using it for any commercial purpose where he would require such advanced features in the phone. Suppose he is utilizing the advanced features just for entertainment; in that case, it's a waste of money. It may bring additional liability and would have an imbalance of income and liabilities and a disturbing lifestyle just for an entertainer.

4. Avoid the burden of new liabilities – No new loans:

Some people opt for a home loan to avoid monthly expenditure on rent, the hustle of shifting the house during a particular period and generating an asset. As the value of your property will increase over a while, it can prove to be a good investment. However, taking an additional loan for interior design, furniture, new TV, new fridge, car etc., will add to your liabilities since you are spending money on entertainment and not on productive things. I am not against spending on these things; however, I suggest paying a surplus or intended amount instead of adding on a new loan. In simple words, such expenditure should have been scheduled in advance.

> *"Easy payments, easy lease, easy approval. Debt is straightforward to get into, but makes it hard to live victoriously."*
> *- Bradley Vinson, Men Get Real With Your Finances.*

5. Settle your loans as early as possible:

Nowadays, you can pay off your loan before time, and no changes/penalties are being levied for early repayment. To settle your loan in less time, you can start paying off additional installments every year or increase your installment premium by some percentage. You can also reduce your burden of paying interest on a home loan by keeping your tenure for a lesser period. Always try to minimize your expenses to pay additional loan installments. In this way, you can pay off your loan in lesser time, and simultaneously you can save money by spending less on interest.

From the following chart, you will understand how an additional contribution and lesser tenure towards your home loan can save your money on the interest portion of the home loan and set you free from the loan at an early stage.

Tenure	Change in interest portion as per the tenure			Change in interest portion on additional contribution at constant tenure			
	25 yrs	20 yrs	15 yrs	25 yrs	25 yrs	25 yrs	25 yrs
Loan Amount	40 lac	40 lac	40 lac	40 lac	40 lac	40 lac	40 lac
Rate Of Int	8%	8%	8%	8%	8%	8%	8%
EMI	30873	30873	30873	30873	30873	30873	30873
Principal Amount Paid	40 lac	40 lac	40 lac	40 lac	40 lac	40 lac	40 lac
Pay Extra EMI Every Yr	0	0	0	1	0	0	1
Hike EMI By _% Every Yr	0	0	0	0	5%	10%	5%
Int. Paid	5261795	3976647	2835127	3979216	2974245	2333918	2642385

reference: https://bit.ly/warikooemicalculator

6. Set priority and cut off the heavy loans first:

Suppose any person has taken various loans that is Home Loan @ 9%, Personal Loan @ 14%, Gold Loan @ 8.5%; Car Loan @ 13%, and Credit Card Loan @ 3% per month; in that case, it is advisable to cut off the heavy loans on top priority. Setting priority includes the loan amount, the repayment criteria, and the tenure. Considering the example of a credit card, they charge a monthly interest rate of 3% on the outstanding amount; as a result, the annual interest rate works out to 36%. In this scenario, paying a credit card loan should be the top priority as a credit card loan is costlier than other loans. Therefore, he should concentrate on clearing the credit card loan with additional installments while paying the regular EMI of different loans.

7.   Timely review of Wealth and Assets:

Timely review of our wealth and assets facilitate us to make decisions about the strategic utilization of our assets to make money for us. For that, one needs to note all the sources of your income and assets, such as available cash, investments, real estate, gift fund, physical gold, etc., on a notable media. It will bring the consciousness about the wealth/assets you possess and make us think about how we can utilize it to produce more money.

> *"The speed of your success is limited only by your dedication and what you're willing to sacrifice." - Nathan W. Morris, Your 33-Day Money Action Plan.*

Chapter 3. How can I earn money with my possessions?

"Geeta, while explaining managing our finances, you have mentioned creating wealth from our possessions. So how can I make our possessions generate more wealth for us" said Seeta.

> "To get rich, you have to be making money while you're asleep." — David Bailey, Wholefood Heaven In A Bowl.

Geeta: If you limit your ability to make money to eight hours a day, you won't find financial freedom. To create wealth, let your money and assets work for you so you can make money while you sleep. You need to find new sources of passive income. As you know, I had bought a car and borrowed it to earn additional income. Here are some examples of passive income.

> Never depend on a single income. Make investments to create a second source. — Warren Buffett, The Intelligent Investor.

1. **Rent your real estate:**

Renting your real estate is the easiest way to create passive income without extra effort, provided you own a property. Suppose you own a home, apartment, or office space, then you can simply rent your property for additional income. If you own land, you can develop it for commercial purposes and rent it for various family functions like marriages, birthdays, parties, etc., for official events, and car parking for any significant event near your property. So it would be better if you think out of the box when it comes to extra space you might have.

2. **Rent your car or commercialize it:**

Renting your car for commercial purposes can create an additional source of income for you. For example, you can rent it out to companies like Ola, Uber, and Zoom car. Likewise, you can make it available for tourists, school/college/office pick up & drop facilities, wedding events, etc Advertising using your car is an another way to generate passive income. Nowadays, many companies are advertising this way, and you can adopt the same with the wrap2earn application on mobile or any other agency.

3. Make your funds create wealth for you:

Investing your money in various forms can create wealth for yourself. Nowadays, interest rates on bank FDs gradually decrease and may fall further. Currently, we can earn only 5 to 6 % simple interest per annum on a fixed deposit with the bank. In addition, fixed deposits come with a specified lock-in period, and if liquidated before maturity, you would be charged the penalty, which affects your returns.

Various available options to invest your hard-earned money in the market to gain better returns than fixed deposits are as follows:

Investment in Mutual Fund:

Investing in mutual funds is one of the best ways to generate passive income. You can choose mutual funds based on your risk appetite and goal. It allows you to create the wealth passively and provides you the freedom to select the time horizon for investments and risk appetite. Mutual fund investments have become an easy tool for investment due to the advancement in technology. You can now invest and track your investments online with any available media like a computer or smartphone. You can start investing in Mutual Funds with as little as Rupees Five Hundred via SIP (Systematic Investment Plan).

Of all the available options or types of Mutual Funds schemes, Debt fund investments are the most preferable to investors with a low to moderate risk appetite. As debt mutual funds do not have a lock-in period, they provide liquidity, allowing you to withdraw your money from the fund scheme on any given business day. On the other hand, equity scheme investments have a proven track record of multiplying the sum invested over the long term. Time plays a vital role in this growth of the sum invested because equity is highly volatile in the short term. One can review the fund performances from various AMC or Money control websites and choose the best suitable fund according to financial goal and time horizon. In addition, one can seek help from a registered investment advisor (RIA) to find the best-suited mutual fund.

Investment in Gold:

Indians are among the world's leading consumers of gold, and this precious metal constitutes a significant portion of our total imports. Indians tend to buy gold since it is considered a 'secure' investment. Moreover, many people purchase gold ornaments in India on various occasions like festivals, weddings, auspicious days, etc. Therefore, it is a known option for investing in gold. However, buying gold ornaments involves 20-30% of the cost, as making charges.

Further, it remains idle and unused as the gold ornaments are being used occasionally; and are predominantly kept in bank lockers. For that reason, it doesn't prove to be a money-making asset; however, one can monetize it in an emergency. Although the value of gold increases over a while, the percentage of appreciation of gold value is minimal compared to the value of gold as a commodity/gold ETF.

Unlike physical gold, one can purchase ETF, like shares on a stock exchange. ETFs allow investors to access gold, avoiding the various costs like making charges, storage cost and inconvenience, , and security risks of holding physical gold. The Gold ETF pricing is uniform to international standards and is always transparent. Gold ETFs have an expense ratio of 1%, and brokerage charges around 0.5% or less. You can also invest in gold shares from the commodity market or the shares of any well-known jeweller listed in the share market.

If you remember, the gold price in 1995 was approx. Rs.5000/- for ten grams, which has increased to Rs.47000/- per 10 grams in 2021. So it means the gold value has increased by 10%.

However, if one had bought one share of Tanishq @ Re.1/- in 1995, it would have become Rs.1500/- in 2021, giving 1500% appreciation.

Investment in the Stock market:

The stock market is another way to generate the passive income. It, of course, is something that requires a certain level of expertise and knowledge. If you have good knowledge about the market, you can start investing in appropriate stocks to gain returns. It is a pretty risky deal but gives high returns. You might be afraid to invest because of the risk. If you have a clear understanding of the stock market, you will be more confident pursuing financial freedom.

> "Risk comes from not knowing what you're doing." — Warren Buffett, The Intelligent Investor.

Certain companies with dividend-yielding stocks believe in distributing a part of their profits to their investors at least once a year. You have to buy the stock and hold it to the market conditions. When disbursing dividends, they get directly credited to your bank account linked to the trading account.

However, you will have to do a good amount of research before picking such stocks that yield dividends. Dividends are paid per share, which means that you earn more dividends if you hold more shares in the company. Suppose you don't have a piece of good knowledge about investing in stocks; in that case, you can obtain the help of a financial investment planner or may go for any training course on share market investing to gain additional income with the expertise.

Here I would like to share an example. An investor had purchased 1000 shares of ITC in the year 2004. The value of 1 share was Rs.1000/- approx.; that means he had invested Rs.10 lac in ITC share in 2004. Those 1000 shares became 45000 shares in 2020 after the share split and bonus shares. In June 2020, the company paid a dividend of Rs.10.15 per share as such income from the dividend in the year 2020 was Rs.4,56,750/- only though dividend and the value of those shares in 16 years is Rs. 92.25 lac. This is the power of compounding. Below are the details of the stock split and bonuses issued by ITC since 2004:

No. of shares compounding	Qty	Total balance Qty
ITC Shares purchased	1000	1000
10:1 Split	9000	10000
1:2 Bonus	5000	15000
1:1 Bonus	15000	30000
1:2 Bonus	15000	45000
Shares in DMAT		45000

The Bottom Line is to get started, since earning more is the gateway to the wealthy lifestyle you have always dreamed of. Once you start making more money, you'll gain control over your life in ways you never thought possible. Of course, it won't always be easy. There is no money-making without a risk involvement; whether starting a business or investing in stocks, every avenue to make money requires some risk. So to earn more, you should learn to take calculated risks. You might get lots of failures in bringing it to happen as calculated, but eventually, you'd realize the secret of earning more money.

> "I believe that financial peace is possible for all of us through knowledge and discipline." - Dave Ramsey, Smart Money Smart Kids.

Seeta, these are a few passive income options from which you may go for convenient selective options that can earn money without any extra effort to earn money. By adopting this, you can make your possessions work for you in making money. Besides this, you may also get into other available passive income options to earn money.

Start Investing by opening DMAT account with Zerodha. Click on the link below to open Zerodha DMAT account:
https://zerodha.com/?c=QL9939&s=CONSOLE

Chapter 4. What are the passive income options?

"What is passive income, Geeta?" Said Seeta

Geeta: Passive income is money earned with a minimal activity that requires little extra effort from an individual. A good passive income idea means you should be able to go out and get a full-time job and still be able to run your passive income streams. Renting your property/possessions is one example of such income. In addition, building multiple passive income streams has an added short-term benefit; it makes you more strong and better able to weather economic shocks. Here are some of the ways to Passive Income:

> *"To obtain financial freedom, one must be either a business owner or an investor or both, generating passive income, particularly every month."* - Robert Kiyosaki.

Writing an eBook

Writing an e-book and publishing has become a popular way to earn passive income. EBooks are incredibly successful on non-fiction topics like online marketing, business development, career advice, personal/professional requirements, etc.

While fiction eBooks are also good sellers, their market is much more competitive than non-fiction ones. Once you've written an eBook, you can put it for sale on online platforms like Amazon's Kindle Direct Publishing or Apple's iTunes Connect.

Writing a Paperback Book

This specific option is for those who think they have enough skill to write a book and take their skill professionally. Then, depending on a selected topic, you just have to spare extra time and effort for writing at least 5-6 days a week. You can expect to get 7% - 12.5% as royalties. An elementary example is if you will price your book at Rs. 200/- and you are set for 10% royalties, and you sell 1000 books a month – you make …. 20,000 a month per book just by sitting at home and doing nothing!

Creating Podcast

These days, people's lives are so fast-paced that multitasking has become the need of the hour. Podcasts have become so popular; they allow people to get information or entertainment while commuting to a job, workouts, cooking, etc. In addition, podcasts are much more accessible than YouTube videos to create and can be shared easily on iTunes. So select a topic that you're well-versed or passionate about, and start a related podcast.

Creating Online Training Courses

Online learning platforms have become highly favorable from the year 2020 onwards due to the COVID pandemic. People use various online platforms to train themselves to enhance their specific interests. Suppose you are familiar with any fields, e.g., web designing, programming, photography, digital marketing, languages, running start-ups, etc. Then, you may create and publish the courses on online platforms and earn money with user subscriptions.

Selling Stock Photos Online

If you are a photographer or enjoy snapping magic moments, you can put that talent to work or bring professionalism! If you want to make money from your habitual skills and the best clicks, you may consider an option to sell your images as stock photos. Many online options are available to upload your clicks for sale as stock images, such as Adobe Stock, Shutterstock, etc. On the other hand, using the skill and additional workforce resources, you may adopt the other earning profession of selling your stock images on your website.

Affiliate marketing

Affiliate marketing is another most straightforward way to make passive income through advertisement and selling products and services. It could involve branding /selling your or a third-party product, or you may consider working for multiple organizations. Many affiliate marketing channels are offerings free joining and provide decent pay-outs for every conversion.

Amazon affiliate marketing is one popular source of making passive income online. You can create content about the products available on Amazon and make money from it. You get paid every time someone purchases from your affiliate link.

YouTube channel

YouTube is a viral social media these days. According to a recent survey in 2019, an average user spends 84 minutes a day watching videos.

People now treat YouTube as a guide to their various queries, be it kids, students, housewives, working professionals, or even a businessman. You may create a YouTube channel about something you find a happening subject, social, personal activities, political subject, or general topics. It could be on reviewing books, movies, websites, etc.

Many people are running their channels and earning an income through YouTube. As always, you'll need to find a niche that isn't yet saturated and focus on making engaging videos. Once you start getting minimum views and subscriptions, your earnings will start. If you could reach the club of videos with 100k+ views, you would benefit from relying on the YouTube video income.

Author's YouTube channel links:
(1493) A*GAMING - YouTube
(12073) Aara's world - YouTube

Writing a Blog

A blog is a cost-effective method to generate an actual passive income. The primary role of starting a blog is to figure out a topic of interest or a popular subject and create valuable content about it. If you maintain the blog consistency to generate value for many interested people, you can generate an extraordinary passive income. Once you start posting the informative articles to your blog regularly, your blog site will be recognized while bringing in traffic whether or not putting extra effort in terms of time and resources. While it sounds easy, it takes initial time and study efforts for the selected subject and digital marketing to start making money from your blog. Based on your topic and dedication, it can take somewhere around 3 to 6 months to get your first passive income.

Author's Blog: Blogger: Posts

Chapter 5. What is the secret behind the success of progressive people?

"Seeta, I have explained how you can get rid of the financial crisis and various ways of generating more money through passive income. However, it is essential to put in consistent efforts to achieve your goals. You set to have massive activeness as progressive people do. Even when progressive people face a setback, they find ways to be constantly motivated but never give up. I follow habitual ways that keep me motivated and strong to handle negative situations", Geeta continued.

> *"The secret to wealth is simple: Find a way to do more for others than anyone else. Become more valuable. Do more. Give more. Be more. Serve more." — Tony Robbins, Money Master the Game: 7 Simple Steps to Financial Freedom.*

Pursuing financial freedom means breaking the status quo. You could no longer live on the 'average,' but you should have a passion for going beyond. This quote reminds us that to build wealth and be successful, we must give, serve, and be a cut above everyone else.

Successful people are planners who think differently or out of the box and act accordingly. They are progressive and always looking ahead to get into new things, so they are habitual succowners. Many people are consumed with past actions, failures, and mistakes; on the other side, progressive people learn from and overcome past failures or errors to achieve success. Therefore, you have to adapt to powerful habits to succeed in life. A few of the powerful habits of progressive people have been described ahead:

Always focus on solutions:

If Progressive people enter into a project and things don't turn out the way they expected, instead of getting involved in the problem, they focus on the possible solutions. They better understand that one can only learn from what didn't work and try to integrate it into a solution. They find possibilities and workarounds to seeming difficult questions through practical and creative thinking.

Find better ways by asking the right questions:

While progressive people focus on solutions, they do well to ask the right questions to boost growth. For example, they would ask, "What did we do wrong?" "What would have been done better?" "How can the sales be improved?"

The right questions always lead to better ways of getting things done and guide you to your desired destination. However, it may require your kind attention to the details or seek support where necessary.

Progressive people are not rigid.

They want results, and whenever they need the support or advice of others to get the things done, they have the readiness to listen to others, whether learning new things or opinions from juniors in terms of age and experience and gain knowledge from every possible source. A successful person challenges to self and keeps trying to be a better version.

Become accustomed to the change :

They are not afraid to change since adaptation is the key to survival and progressive people are excellent at adapting. When you learn to adapt, you focus on doing only the necessary things to achieve results.

Take responsibility without any excuses :

If things don't work out as planned, they know that it is up to them to act and find the possible ways to get results. Therefore, they don't believe or produce any excuses for the success path and don't carry any intentions to play the blame game.

Look for the best in others :

It's a theory that the surrounding people always try to disappoint you, and unfortunately, you have been mistreated because we don't live in a picture-perfect world. Yet Progressive people can have a decent attitude in every situation and hope to see the best in those they are dealing with. So while retrogressive people think or assume that everyone is trying to take them down, progressives discover the strength in those they come across and use it for the good of everyone.

They know when to let go :

You need the things to leave for nothing, and leaving doesn't mean a failure but can be a strength. However, you have to timeline the things to keep them aside. Progressive people know or better streamline the progress and calculate the odds by keeping such things aside or letting them go and move ahead towards success. It is a significant factor in growth and acceptance.

Maintain values :

Progressive people wouldn't compromise their standards to please the crowd; instead, they will safeguard their values and principles. As a result, their values evolve into a compass or guide to help them achieve their set goals and adopt their character.

Chapter 6. Money Mind Block?

Like Seeta, billions of people have a negative belief about money. Trust that holds them back from getting rich. This negative limiting belief hinders their financially successful life and makes them live an ordinary life.

Now you must be thinking about the topic - What Are Money Blocks? And how they hold us back from getting rich. So here is the answer! Money blocks are commonly known as negative limiting beliefs that stand in the way of your financial goals. Some of the negative money blocks/views of people have been explained here to give more clarity about negative money blocks:

Getting rich is not my cup of tea:

Financial freedom starts with having the right mindset to pursue wealth and audacious goals. This quote reminds us that rich people have an active role in designing their dream life.

> "Rich people believe 'I create my life.' Poor people believe 'Life happens to me.'"— T. Harv Eker, Secrets of the Millionaire Mind: Mastering the Inner Game of Wealth

Some people believe that one needs to be lucky to become rich; I am not good enough; I do not have much potential to get rich. This belief would never allow them to make extra efforts to become rich. They keep doing their regular 9-5 jobs and saving a little money for the future. They never think out of the box to change their lives.

On the other hand, wealthy people believe that they can create wealth even if the conditions are not in their favour. Therefore, they always think out of the box and take action towards getting rich. Since they believe they are born to get rich, their behavior becomes like that, taking them towards the manifestation of their dreams. Dhirubhai Ambani, Shahrukh Khan, and Rajnikanth are some of the examples who rose from nothing, bypassed the obstacles, and proved themselves as successful person.

Another example who has bypassed the obstacles and proved herself as a successful person is

Kalpana Saroj, born in Roper kheda village in Maharashtra. Kalpana Saroj's life is one of the extraordinary successes against all odds. At the age of 12, she was married off by her parents and subsequently faced physical abuse at the hands of her husband and his parents. She tried committing suicide but then was taken in by her uncle at 16. Taking loans that the government-sanctioned for people born under the Scheduled Caste community, she started her own sewing business. When it became a success, she started a furniture business. Soon, it would buy the assets of Kamani Tubes Company and turn the loss-making company into a very lucrative business.

Money is the root cause of all evil. It brings anxiety and sleepless nights:

Some people believe that whoever is rich, has huge money; faces problems such as anxiety, sleepless night, fear of robbery, income tax, etc., so it's better to enjoy life with whatever money we earn. Therefore, they tend to sacrifice their financial well-being and become barriers to their financial success.

On the other hand, the wealthiest people see money as a tool that provides more options and opportunities for growth and the well-being of society. Mukesh Ambani, Ratan Tata is the example of the wealthiest people in India; however, they do not face any trouble because of money but have brought more power to them.

Money doesn't grow on trees.

Many people grow up listening to this sentence from their childhood and start believing in that. They think that money is hard to earn and they need to work hard to make money, no one can earn money quickly, and thus they get the same outcome as they believe. On the other hand, wealthy people believe that money is easy to make because they relish their work, have unique ideas, and love collaborating, creating, and doing the right things. All you need to do is constantly work on setting goals with passion and hard work.

> *"Nobody can predict the future, but one can surely work towards building it."*

Here is the story of two brothers: Bhavin Turakhia and Divyank Turakhia - the real example.

Bhavin Turakhia and Divyank Turakhia have built approximately a dozen companies in their one and a half years of career, out of which Directi is their base company. After selling their five companies, these brothers were listed on India's richest person list by Forbes in 2016.

Born and brought up in Mumbai, these brothers started working towards their dreams at thirteen. Divyank Turakhia had a long-lasting love for coding since his childhood. So he built his first game with his brother to track the growth and prices of the stock market. After developing this game, his interest in coding grew day by day, making it challenging to study. So his father began convincing Divyank to enroll in the program B.Com. But, to keep his father's words, Divyank had taken admission for the same but never attended college as his interest was in coding, not B.com. So all day long, they used to stay home and learn to code, and when they had enough grip on coding, in 1998, they decided to start their own company.

For the start-up capital, they convinced their father, and he gave them Rs. 25000 / - to start the business. With this start-up capital, Bhavin

Turakhia started his first company Directi at the age of 18, together with his brother Divyank Turakhia at the age of 16, built a web hosting company that provides website domain names and internet services to other companies. Then they built another famous Bigrock company under the same flag. After that, they launched ten more companies under the same banner Directi.

Currently, Directi has more than 1,000 employees and 10 million customers around the globe.
In 2014, Bhavin and Divyank Turakhia sold four of their companies- Logic Boxes, Bigrock, Webhosting.info, and Reseller Club, to the US-Based web hosting company Endurance International Group for $160 Million. Last year, they sold another company, Media.net- Adsense company, founded in 2010, to a Chinese company for $900 Million.

Keep your money safe :

Some people are extremely conservative with their finances. They always have a fear mindset of losing money and can't recover the invested capital. They always have a deep focus on saving their hard-earned money; as a result, they don't dare to take the risk of money growth through investments. Thus, they could not step up in life, whereas wealthy people always take the potential risk of knowing the effect of gains & losses. They make their money to work for them, giving more money in return. They always study and track their investments and profit-loss for better understanding. Rakesh Jhunjhunwala, Warren Buffet, and Radhakrishna Damani are some examples.

Here's the story of Rakesh Jhunjhunwala.

Rakesh Jhunjhunwala, also known as the "Indian Warren Buffett" or "big bull," was born on 5th July 1960 in Mumbai. His father was an income tax official.

Rakesh Jhunjhunwala always heard his father talking to his friends about shares. He was very curious about shares, so he once asked his father why the share price fluctuated daily. His father suggested reading newspapers as the news makes the stock prices fluctuate.

RakeshJhunjhunwala also expressed his wish to pursue a career in the stock market. However, his father suggested that he get a graduate degree from a college. So then, in 1985, Rakesh Jhunjhunwala graduated from Sydenham College as a Chartered Accountant.

After graduation, he discussed his career goal as a stock market investor with his father again. His father permitted him to pursue any career.; however, he also added that he's not going to give him any money, nor would he ask for the initial capital from his father's friends.

Mr. Rakesh Jhunjhunwala started his career in the stock market with just Rs.5000/- in 1985. Sensex stood at 150 points (currently, Sensex is around 50,000 points). According to the latest Forbes updates, Rakesh Jhunjhunwala's net worth is $3.1 billion, equating to more than Rs. 19000 Cr.

Working hard at a job will make me rich :

Most people entrust their job even if they are not satisfied and stick to it till retirement. The common thinking for the working professionals includes regular income & stability, yearly increments, various allowances, and yearly performance bonuses, and by saving apart from this hard-earned money, they can become rich and fulfill dreams. On the other hand, wealthy people work for their passion; they find the job they love and work with intensity & excellence. As a result, they get rewarded with healthy wealth. M S Dhoni, Sachin Tendulkar and Sushant Singh Rajput are the examples we have.

> "Working because you want to, not because you have to, is financial freedom." - Tony Robbins.

Another famous example is Narayana Murthy. He is the founder of Infosys, also known as the IT sector's father, the man with a net worth of $1.9 billion, a person who doesn't need any introduction, a self-made man, and his work speaks aloud. But life wasn't that easy for

Narayana Murthy as he wasn't from the wealthy family background. He was as normal as we were, but the only difference from other ordinary people was that his confidence was powerful; he had a burning desire to achieve what he had always dreamed of. He was determined and hardworking; he didn't want it, but he decided and took action accordingly to fulfill his dreams. He didn't give up until he didn't achieve his goals; he faced every struggle and difficulty with courage and strength.

After he completed engineering, he started working in the Indian Institute of Management in Ahmedabad as a chief system programmer; around the 70s, he started his First own Entrepreneurial venture, Named Softronics, a software consulting firm. However, after about a year, his company sadly failed and had to shut down; because of this disastrous situation,

Narayana was left with no option, and he had to take a job. Hence he joined an IT firm Named Patni Computer systems in Pune.

While working at Patni, Narayana's mind was still on his passion for entrepreneurship; he knew he belonged to entrepreneurship. He had a strong will that he wanted for it, passionate about making his software of excellent quality. But the big problem he faced was the lack of money, but his passion did not allow him to give up. He was so passionate that his wife understood his pain and the fact that he wanted to achieve something great in his life, but the only thing stopping him was money.

Looking at Narayana's passion and burning desire, his wife Sudha also decided to support him. She gave a complete relaxation from household responsibilities, including expenditure, additionally backed with a cash holding of Rs.1000/-.

After getting financial and family support, one day, Narayana met his six engineering colleagues in his apartment to officially discuss forming a software company based on software coding. After discussion, Narayana decided to take a step forward towards his dream by a dare decision to leave a well-settled job at Patni and concentrate on his dream project. With immediate action, significant hard work, efforts, and aggressive preparation, INFOSYS, formerly known as Infosys Consultants Private Limited, was registered on 2nd July 1981. Today, it is one of the top IT companies.

Formal education can make you rich :

Most people or from the heard sources strongly believe that formal education is the key to a wealthy life and that excellent grades in education may lead to a better job with a handsome salary to make them wealthy. But, on the other side, rich people give their extra efforts in gaining constructive knowledge and try to bring excellence to achieve thee success where others lag; where money and fame are the by-products. Sachin Tendulkar, Lata Mangeshkar, and Dhirubhai Ambani are the famous names who achieved the milestones with no higher educational background but are the masters in their skills and professions, making them successful personalities.

Another example is an Indian entrepreneur and businessman, Prem Ganapathy, who founded the trendy chain of restaurants called the Dosa Plaza. But his beginnings were humble; being one of the seven children in a poor household in Tamil Nadu and having completed his 10th grade; he set off to Mumbai to follow success. With the help of a Tamil family who took pity on him and offered him a job working in a small bakery. But with genuine efforts, planning, and a strong mindset, just two years later, he could start his dosa selling a business, which now is a brand among the Dosa Plaza across the world, including New Zealand, Oman, and even UAE!

Chapter 7. The Success Mantra

We have reached to the end of this book with all the facts and the described justification in the previous chapter. So, here's giving a success mantra to become a wealthier version of you.

Get a Perfect Mindset for Money Management :

We all have a powerful asset called "Mind," which plays an important role, especially in money management. One can't develop or make firm financial decisions, keeping you in common unstable living conditions. However, you can change yourself from a poor to a wealthy mindset by adapting and developing financially verified habits.

A popular way to keep your mindset rich, strong, and motivated, you must have a visionary board in the noticeable area. This board would have all the motivational content, including pictures, quotes, your financial goals, etc. It will keep you reminded and boost every day and keep you motivated enough to step towards achieving the desired financial goal sets.

Another simple way to boost your money mindset is to read financially prosperous persons' success stories or biographies. It will benefit you to challenge and overcome any struggling situation to achieve the milestone.

Take bold moves to become rich :

It's an ambitious goal to become a wealthy person, and if you're aiming for that, do something big and make some significant life changes. Exploit your skills and invest in making self-employed expertise.

Make it a goal to have a step ahead of others. Work on it, learn it, train it, practice, evaluate and refine it. The success reason for most millionaire sports players or entertainers is their utilization of self-skills to develop to make them different from others. If there's something you're good at, it is likely you can reap considerable rewards from it.

Always spend time with people who force you to level up :

Surroundings make a huge difference when it comes to financial success. Remember the famous quote by Jim Rohn,

> *"You are the average of the five people you spend the most time with."?.... Jim Rohn*

All of us are mutually influenced by the people around us, especially by the close ones with whom we spend the maximum time, i.e., friends, office colleagues, family members, mentors, etc. Such people are majorly considered or regularly accompanied to create, develop, and mentor, creating a better financial status and adversely demoralizing or downfall.

You must seek certain qualities of your mentor. Be sure that a selective friend circle accompanies you. It is believed that if you have certain blind spots or a specific ambition in life, get with those people who would likely have the potential to fill out these gaps and whose intentions are to boost your efforts towards success. Being with such a group of people means raising expectations and building that ability to learn their positive side on your own.

Keep yourself away from grudges :

Forgiveness is also essential part of life but underestimated. People should learn to forgive others coming across your success path or knowingly putting obstacles in any possible ways to keep you down. Learn to forgive the one who is the reason for setting you back, and once accomplished, the win is yours.

While you achieve to clear all the money blocks in your life, at the same time, do the practice of writing about the list of money blocking beliefs you came across till day and continue it without any interruption. Then review it when you have a feeling of achievement. Finally, read all the experiences aloud to feel the emotions and say, "I forgive, love you, and I'm sorry, thank you." You'll feel relaxed by the end of the list by lifting the weight off your shoulders.

Be Thankful :

Not the last, but one more underestimated tool is giving thanks for everything in your life, whether your one-time gains, present or even will receive in the coming future. Gratitude is the highest frequency for attraction, and the faithful follower becomes a magnet.

I know people may find it hard to get into this practice, but just like any new practice, it would take time to make it habitual. So, to make it easy, I always start with the people in my life that I'm most grateful for and love about their good things. It seems enough to get the momentum going and move forward into the thankful items received in the past, present, and future. It's the best possible way to ensure success.

Grow with others' success :

Undoubtedly, the fastest way to achieve success is to help others succeed. Yet, n the business world, there seems to be a belief that the only way to get ahead is to watch out for number one but practically is not as simple as it seems. In the best words, Brian Tracy explained,

> *"Successful people are always looking for opportunities to help others. Unsuccessful people are always asking, 'What's in it for me?'" .... Brian Tracy*

The fact is that our greatest successes in life often come from helping others to succeed. If done without any argument when you focus on assisting others, your eventual payoff will always be far greater than your investment.

It's easy to focus time and energy on your corresponding requirements. However, that self-focus can increase only when you face personal or professional challenges. It would be better if you had a deep thought about what needs to be done and worked harder or faster to get through a difficult period. You might have to cut yourself off from friends and community, saying you'll get back to them when things take a better turn.

But what happens if you take the opposite approach? What do you do when you help others, even if you're not sure? You can take the form of volunteering at a local charity or simply helping a colleague at work when you don't need it.

> *"We make a living by what we get. We make a life by what we give." — Winston Churchill.*

Research shows that helping and giving can make you feel connected, have better-growing options, and even live longer.

www.ingramcontent.com/pod-product-compliance
Lightning Source LLC
Chambersburg PA
CBHW070305220526

45465CB00004B/1748